Greater Than a

Nairobi

Kenya

50 Travel Tips from a Local

Mildred Achoch

Lock Haven, PA

All rights reserved.

ISBN: 9781521987193

> TOURIST

Mildred Achoch

BOOK DESCRIPTION

Are you excited about planning your next trip?

Do you want to try something new while traveling?

Would you like some guidance from a local?

If you answered yes to any of these questions, then this book is just for you.

Greater than a Tourist - Nairobi by Mildred Achoch offers the inside scope on Nairobi. Most travel books tell you how to travel like a tourist. Although there's nothing wrong with that, as a part of the Greater than a Tourist series, this book will give you travel tips from someone who lives at your next travel destination.

In these pages you'll discover local advice that will help you throughout your stay. This book will not tell you exact addresses or store hours but instead will give you an excitement and knowledge from a local that you may not find in other smaller print travel books. Travel like a local. Slow down, stay in one place, and get to know the people and the culture of a place.

By the time you finish this book, you will be eager and prepared to travel to your next destination.

Mildred Achoch

TABLE OF CONTENTS

16. Stop Over At The Nairobi Gallery

17. Explore 90 year old Mcmillan Library

18. Sample The Arts At Alliance Francaise

19. Feed The Giraffes At The Giraffe Centre

20. Feed An Elephant At The Elephant Orphanage

21. Embrace Mother Nature At Karura Forest

22. Honour The Fallen At The Nairobi War Cemetery

23. Explore The Kenya National Archives

24. Activate Your Artivism at Pawa 254

25. Go Racing At The GP Karting

26. Learn Some Sheng Words

27. Watch A Play At The Kenya National Theatre

28. Stay At The Flora Hostel

29. Get Techy At The IHub

30. Experience Kenyan And German Arts At Goethe

31. Eat Kenyan Cuisine At Mama Oliech Restaurant

32. Stay At The Flora Hostel

33. Sample Swahili Cuisine At Swahili Plate

34. Test Your Aim At The Kenya Rifle Club

35. Enjoy The Blues At The Blues

36. Go Horse Riding At Malo Stables

37. Attend The Madaraka Day Celebrations

38. Get Entertained At The Drama Festival

39. Watch A Football Match At A Nairobi Stadium

DEDICATION

This book is dedicated to my mother, Anastasia Wacera Achoch and my father, Edwin Sport Achoch. Thank you for everything. I miss you both.

Mildred Achoch

ABOUT THE AUTHOR

Mildred Achoch is a screenwriter, poet and Christian Goth who was born, raised and still lives in Nairobi, Kenya. She loves films and rock 'n' roll so it is not surprising that she is the founder of ROFFEKE – Rock 'n' Roll Film Festival, Kenya.

Mildred Achoch

HOW TO USE THIS BOOK

This book was written by someone who has lived in an area for over three months. The author has made the best suggestions based on their own experiences in the area. Please check that these places are still available before traveling to the area. The goal of this book is to help travelers either dream or experience different locations by providing opinions from a local.

Mildred Achoch

FROM THE PUBLISHER

Traveling can be one of the most important moments in a person's life. The memories that you have of anticipating going somewhere new or getting to travel are some of the best. As a publisher of the Greater Than a Tourist book series, as well as the popular 50 Things to Know book series, we strive to help you learn about new places, spark your imagination, and inspire you.

Thought this book you will find something for every traveler. Wherever you are and whatever you do I wish you safe fun, and inspiring travel.

Lisa Rusczyk Ed. D.
CZYK Publishing

Mildred Achoch

WELCOME TO > TOURIST

Mildred Achoch

INTRODUCTION

Nairobi is the capital city of Kenya. The word "Nairobi" is Maasai in origin and means "place of cool waters". Nairobi is also known as "The Green City in the Sun" due to the forest cover that is found in various parts of the city. Such green areas include Lang'ata, where the only National Park located in a city can be found; Karen, the area named after Karen Blixen, whose life story was immortalized in the Oscar winning movie, "Out of Africa" and Kilimani, where the Nairobi Arboretum is located.

Kibera, one of the largest slums in the world and the location of the award-winning Kenyan film "Soul Boy", is from the Nubian name "Kibra" which means jungle or forest. Unlike in Kibera, where there isn't much forest cover remaining, Karura forest is made up of over 1000 hectares of indigenous trees and plantations and is home to over 600 wildlife species.

This book will give you some handy tips about the above-mentioned areas and other fascinating places that you can visit in Nairobi.

Mildred Achoch

1. Learn The Basics of Nairobi

English is the official language in Kenya and Swahili is the national language so these two are widely spoken in Nairobi. Sheng – a mixture of English, Kiswahili and vernacular languages – is also spoken, especially by younger people. About 70 percent of Kenya's population is made up of young people and this is also reflected in the city's population. Nairobi is a melting pot of cultures; you will interact with Africans, Indians, the descendants of the British and various Europeans. The weather is pleasant most of the year with the dry/hot season between December and Feburary and the cold season between June and August.

2. Beware of Nairobi Traffic

Nairobi is a bustling city and the traffic can be extremely heavy, especially during weekdays. You will be arriving at the Jomo Kenyatta International Airport which is located about 16 kilometres from the city centre. Here's a tip: time your arrival in Nairobi to coincide with the weekend. Late Friday night is highly recommended. Alternatively, you can time your arrival to coincide with a public holiday, except just before and during Christmas, Easter and New Year since most Nairobians travel during this time. The other major holidays are Labour Day (May 1st), Madaraka Day (June 1st), Mashujaa Day (October 20th) and Jamhuri Day (December 12th).

3. Commute by Matatu

To get around the city like a true Nairobian, you need to board a matatu. Matatus are colourful, flamboyant, loud minibuses that are a central part of the Nairobi youth culture. On the outside, they are covered with graffiti-inspired artwork and flash lights. Inside, loud hiphop, reggae or Kenyan music blares. Some matatus have flat screen TVs inside showing music videos. Some even have free onboard wifi. Tip: Be sure to have smaller denominatons of money to pay the matatu fare.

4. Learn Some Swahili Phrases

Swahili is widely spoken in Nairobi so it will be helpful to know a few Swahili phrases. Hello is habari, good morning is habari ya asubuhi, good evening is habari ya jioni, goodbye is kwaheri, yes is ndio, no is hapana, okay is sawa, thank you is asante, please is tafadhali, welcome is karibu, samahani is excuse me, sorry is pole, I don't have is sina, I want is nataka, how much is pesa ngapi, there isn't any is hakuna and of course no worries is hakuna matata, as immortalized in the popular animation film the Lion King! Tip: You can learn Swahili in one week at the National Museum, in an intensive 20 hour course.

5. Explore the Nairobi National Park

The Nairobi National Park is located about 30 kilometres from the airport and only 7 kilometres from the city centre. This makes it stand out because there is nowhere else in the whole world where you will find a protected area that is this close to a capital city. You will spend the whole day in the Park, enjoying the wide variety of wild animals that you will see during the Safari walk and later, during the game drive. Then you will spend the night in the Nairobi Tented Camp, located right inside the Nairobi National Park.

6. Go Back In Time At The Karen Blixen Museum

The Karen Blixen Museum is located 10 kilometres from the city centre and is about 20 kilometres from the Nairobi National Park. It was once the centre piece of a farm that was owned by Danish Author Karen and her Swedish Husband, Baron Bror von Blixen Fincke. The oscar-winning film, "Out of Africa", which was based on Karen's autobiography, was shot here. The guided tour will take you back in time, where you will be able to see such intimate artifacts like the lantern that Karen hung on her veranda to let her lover, Denys Hatton, know that she was home. You can also see her ill-fated lover's monogrammed books still on the shelves.

7. Visit The Wilson Airport

The Wilson Airport is about 13 kilometres from the Karen Blixen Museum. Although it has lost a little bit of its "wildness", Wilson Airport is still leafy, enticing and a bit eccentric; definitely not boring like your typical, sterile international airport! Tip: arrive by lunchtime so that you can visit the Aero Club. Although it is a private members' organization, they do allow visitors in during lunchtime. The walls are filled with memorabilia from Wilson's past golden age. There are faces of great aviators and their successes and also newspaper cuttings of crashes and the obituaries of the crash victims. David, Karen Blixen's lover, was one such unfortunate victim.

8. Get Educated and Humbled at Kibera

A tour to one of the biggest slums in the world is an educational and humbling experience. You will see a different side of Nairobi, one that many tourists don't know about or are afraid to experience. With a guide who is knowledgable, the Kibera tour will turn out to be the highlight of your trip. Tip: Carry loose demonimations to buy different products from the various entrepreneurs selling their wares along the way, be respectful and take photos only after asking permission from the subjects.

9. Eat Like A Carnivore At The Carnivore

Do you fancy having an endless supply of meat for your gastronomic pleasure? Well, then the aptly named Carnivore is the place for any meat lover. You will be supplied with an endless array of meat and be given a white flag that, when you feel you cannot have even one more piece of meat, you can put the flag down on the table as a sign of defeat – or satisfaction, depending on how you look at the situation! Tip: If you are vegetarian or have a vegetarian companion then ask for the vegetarian menu.

10. See Kenyan Homesteads At The Bomas of Kenya

If you want to experience the whole of Kenyan in just a few hours then the Bomas (homesteads) of Kenya is the pace to visit. At the Bomas of Kenya, you will not only see the various homesteads of many of the 44 tribes of Kenya, you will also have a chance to watch several traditional dances by various tribes, which take place in the afternoons. During the weekdays, the dances begin at 2.30 pm and during the weekends and public holidays, they begin at 3.30pm. Tip: since the Bomas of Kenya is quite near to the Nairobi National Park, you can combine the two trips; tour the park in the morning then visit the Bomas in the afternoon and evening.

11. Visit The Maasai Market

The Maasai market is the go-to place for Kenyan curios and artifacts such as paintings, jewellery, décor items, cutltery, clothes, wallets, sandals and more. Like the Kenyan tribe that it takes its name from, this open-air market is nomadic in nature. On different days of the week, it relocates to different locations in Nairobi. On Saturday and Sunday, the Maasai market is at the city centre, in the High Court parking lot. On weekdays, it is in particular malls around Nairobi. The market takes a break on Mondays. Tip: Don't settle for the first price that is mentioned. Negotiate with the seller to get a better price.

12. Visit The Shangilia Skatepark

Shangilia Skatepark, Kenya's first Multifunctional skatepark, is off Waiyaki Way in Westlands, Nairobi. If you are a skateboarder or a skateboarding fan then this place is worth checking out. It is open from 3pm to 6pm on Mondays to Fridays and all day till 6pm on Saturdays and /Sundays. Tip: Visit the Shangilia orphanage too and spend some time with the orphans.

13. Get Enchanted At Kitengela Hot Glass Limited

For a perfect day out, visit the enchanting world of Kitengela Hot Glass to view glassblowing and dale de verre artisans. The four pillars that Kitengela Hot Glass stands on are creativity, community, consciousness and recycling. It is located on the edge of the Nairobi National Park, on Magadi road, near Ongata Rongai and past Africa Nazarene University. Tip: Catch the glass blowing demonstrations from 9am to noon and 1pm to 4pm on Tuesdays to Saturdays, on Mondays from 8am to noon and 9am to 1pm on Sundays.

Mildred Achoch

Baada ya dhiki faraja (After hardship comes relief) - Swahili Proverb

Mildred Achoch

14. Visit The National Museum

If you would like to learn about Kenyan history and see a wonderful collection of East African birds, then the National Museum is the place to visit. It is located near the Central Busiess District so it is accessible both by public transport and private transport. It is open every day, including the weekends and all public holidays, from 8.30am to 5.30pm. Tip: Give yourself about 4 hours to experience all that the museum has to offer.

15. Travel back in time at the Railway Museum

The Nairobi Railway museum is adjacent to the Nairobi
Railway station. Here, you can see exhibits from the East
African Railway, including different locomotives and a
manual calculating machine that was used in the late 1920s.
You can also see a carriage where an occupant was attacked
by a Tsavo man-eating lion, the train that was used in the
filming of the Oscar-winning movie "Out of Africa" and also,
the chair that was used by the Queen in the 1950s plus the
cups and plates she used. Tip: Use your imagination as there
are no signs, detailed information about the trains or guided
tours around the museum.

16. Stop Over At The Nairobi Gallery

The Nairobi Gallery is located in the Central Business District. It was built in 1913 to house the office of the Provincial Commissioner. It was known as "Hatches, Matches and Dispatches" because of the birth, the marriages and the deaths that were recorded there. Tip: After the tour, you can enjoy great coffee, sandwiches and pastries at the Pointzero Coffee located right at the Nairobi Gallery.

17. Explore 90 year old Mcmillan Library

The 1931 Nairobi blue stone building that houses the McMillan Memorial Library is one of the largest and oldest in Nairobi. It was built by lady McMillan in honour of her husband who hosted notable men such as President Theordore Roosevelt and Winston Churchill. Outside, you will see its beautiful exterior architecture where the front entrance is guarded by stone lion sculptures and inside you will find an extensive Africana section that includes portraits of African soldiers dating 1946, complete with their names. Tip: You can combine a trip to the Nairobi Gallery and the Mcmillan Memorial Library since the two are within a 10-minute walking distance to each other.

18. Sample The Arts At Alliance Francaise

One of the values of the Alliance Francaise is "respect for cultural diversity and a passion for exchanges and diversity." To this end, the Nairobi Alliance Francaise is a hub of cultural diversity and cultural exchange. There are frequent music shows, art exhibitions, film screenings and theatre productions. Tip: You can download the Nairobi program of activities from their website, www. allaincefrnairobi.org

19. Feed The Giraffes At The Giraffe Centre

The Giraffe centre was begun by the grandson of a Scottish earl and is now home to the endangered Rothschild giraffe which is only found in the East Africa region. Thanks to a raised observation platform, you will be able to feed the giraffes yourself as you look at them eye to eye. Tip: if you would like to feed the giraffes from your breakfast table or your bedroom window, then book to stay at the Giraffe Manor, a privately hosted hotel that is located at the Giraffe Centre.

20. Feed An Elephant At The Elephant Orphanage

The David Sheldrick Wildlife Trust, commonly referred to as the Elephant Orphanage, is the place to be during feeding time for baby elephants who have lost their mothers. If you become a foster donor, you will have the privilege of booking in advance to see the baby elephants in the evening too. Tip: In order to get a good viewing spot, be sure to get there early because it is open to the general population for only one hour each day and many people want to see the baby elephants being fed.

21. Embrace Mother Nature At Karura Forest

If you would like to go hiking, biking, jogging or just enjoy some peace and quiet in Mother nature's arms, then Karura Forest is the place to visit. Also, you can see the sacred caves where the Mau Mau freedom fighters hid during Kenya's fight for independence from colonial rule. There is also a 50-foot waterfall and various birds, animals and reptiles. Tip: There are many picnic benches so you can pack a picnic basket then enjoy a lovely picnic break halfway through your hike or bike riding.

22. Honour The Fallen At The Nairobi War Cemetery

Due to its history as the centre of British East Africa, Nairobi did serve as the operational headquarters for a number of campaigns during the first and second World Wars. The Nairobi War Cemetery is located off Ngong road, is the biggest war cemetery in East Africa and is the resting place for about 2000 soldiers. It is very well kept and looks like a scene right out of a Hollywood military cemetery scene. Tip: Explore the headstone inscriptions; many of them will give you much to think about.

23. Explore The Kenya National Archives

At the Kenya National Archives, you will find an interesting collection of historical artifacts such as tribal weapons, masks and handicrafts. There is also a postage stamp exhibit and a reading room where you can peruse through historical documents and books. Tip: Go to the Kenya National Archives on weekdays, 8am to 5pm, since it is closed on weekends.

Mildred Achoch

Haba na haba hujaza kibaba

(Little by little fills up the measure)

– Swahili Proverb

Mildred Achoch

24. Activate Your Artivism at Pawa 254

Pawa 254 believes in Artivism, that is, using art to promote social justice. It is a space where creative people from all sectors meet, create and network. Various events are held there such as art exhibitions, photo exhibitions, spoken word, music concerts, talks and dance shows.

25. Go Racing At The GP Karting

GP Karting's racing track is located not far from the Carnivore restaurant, along Langata road and is open every day from 9am to 6pm except on Mondays when it is closed. Once there, you will be provided with a helmet, racing suit and the full driver's briefing. The computerized timing system will allow you to monitor your lap times. Tip: There is a Sports Bar and Restaurant where you can eat and drink in between the racing and after you have completed racing.

26. Learn Some Sheng Words

Sheng is widely spoken by young people in Nairobi. It is a mixture of English, Swahili and vernacular languages and keeps evolving over time. Some common Sheng phrases include:Ni aje? (How are you/How is the going?) and someone replies with "Poa" (Cool.) or Sasa? (How are you?) and someone replies with "Fiti (Fine). Chapaa is money, Ndai is car, Manzi is a girl and Mangware is very early in the morning.

27. Watch A Play At The Kenya National Theatre

The Kenya National Theatre has been around since the colonial times and is now home to many Kenyan thespians and musicians. There are frequent productions of both contemporary and classic plays plus special events such as music concerts and films screenings. It was recently refurbished, making it a state of the art entertainment venue.

28. Stay At The Flora Hostel

The Flora Hostel is cheap, clean and conveniently located near the Central Business District. Single, double and triple rooms are available all year round except during the annual vacation from December 22nd to Januray the third. It is a Christian-based organization so do not expect non-Christian entertainment.

29. Get Techy At The IHub

If you are interested in technology, innovation and entrepreneurship-related topics and events, then iHub is the place to visit. IHub has hosted fireside chats, entrepreneurs forum discussions, open talks and panels. Tip: check the iHub website (ihub.co.ke) to find out which events will coincide with your trip.

30. Experience Kenyan And German Arts At Goethe

The Goethe Institut is Germany's cultural institute that is active all over the world, including in Kenya. The institute encourages international cultural exchange which is why it is a great place to visit to view art exhibitions, plays, literature-related events, book launches, music shows, film screenings and many other art events. Tip: visit their website to download the programme of activites for the quarter you will be travelling to Nairobi.

31. Eat Kenyan Cuisine At Mama Oliech Restaurant

Mama Oliech Restaurant is the place to eat authentic, tasty, pocket-friendly Kenyan cuisine, such as ugali, local vegetables and its renowned fried Tilapia. When Facebook founder, Mark Zuckerberg, visited Kenya in 2016, he ate at Mama Oliech's after it was recommended to him. He said that he "enjoyed ugali and a whole fried tilapia for the first time and loved them both!" Tip: be sure to get there early before it gets full with the lunch hour crowd.

32. Stay At The Flora Hostel

The Flora Hostel is cheap, clean and conveniently located near the Central Business District. Single, double and triple rooms are available all year round except during the annual vacation period from December 22nd to January 3rd. Tip: It's a Christian-based organization so do not expect non-Christian amenities/entertainment.

33. Sample Swahili Cuisine At Swahili Plate

You don't have to go to the Coastal area of Kenya to treat your tastebuds to the heaven that is Swahili Cuisine. At Swahili Plate, you can sample cuisine that is influenced by Arabic, Indian and European culture. Some of the foods that you can eat include samosa - a fried pastry filled with beef or chicken, mandazi – a popular deep fried pastry, kaimati – fried dumpling coated with a syrup that gives this sweet snack its name, bhajia – fried potatoes that are coated with spices, pilau – spiced rice, biriyani and kachumbari. Tip: Depending on your location, you can choose to go to either the Swahili Plate located at Muindi Mbingu street or the one located at Prestige Plaza along Ngong road.

34. Test Your Aim At The Kenya Rifle Club

The Kenya Regiment Rifle Club is located in Langata, at the Sailing Club. It is equipped with an indoor shooting range, complete with different types of firearms. For less than a dollar, you will get 30 rounds of ammunition. 3 bull's eyes, all the necessary equipment like earmuffs to protect you from the sound of the guns as you shoot and an instructor to assist you if you are a beginner.

Mildred Achoch

Heri kujikwaa kidole kuliko ulimi

(Better to stumble with toe than tongue)

– Swahili Proverb

Mildred Achoch

35. Enjoy The Blues At The Blues

The Blues is located in Barclays Plaza, on Loita Street, not too far from the Alliance Francaise and the Goethe Institut and is open every day from 8am to around 11pm. Part of the mission of The Blues bar and restaurant is to "forge and spread the Blues concept" in Kenya. At the Blues, you can enjoy beautiful and moving blues music – either live or on video – as you eat quality meals and refreshing drinks.

36. Go Horse Riding At Malo Stables

Malo stables offers a horse riding tour of Nairobi where you will be able to enjoy picturesque views of the Ngong Hills as you horse ride from the Karen area into Dagoretti forest. The breakfast horseback trail rides begin at around 8am and end one hour later, after which you will be treated to a sumptuous breakfast in the Karen Blixen house. You can also opt for the Sundowner horseback trail ride which includes one hour of horse riding followed by champagne, soda or any other drink of your choice seated outside around a big tree at the Malo stables yard.

37. Attend The Madaraka Day Celebrations

Madaraka Day (freedom day) is held every June 1st and commemorates the anniversary of when Kenya got internal self-rule from the British colonial government. The day is usually celebrated with pomp and ceremony at either the Nyayo National Stadium or at Uhuru park. You will be treated to traditional dances, military displays and performances by talented artists from all over the country. Tip: Carry some snacks and drinking water.

38. Get Entertained At The Drama Festival

The Kenya schools and colleges drama festival is an annual event that takes place in Kenya from January to April and begins from the zonal level then to the county level, then to the regional level (Nairobi is in the Metropolitan region) and finally to the national level. It is the biggest educational theatre event in the whole of Africa and has produced many young people who are talented in the arts, theater, drama and music. Tip: Find out first where the venue of the regional competitions will be taking place.

39. Watch A Football Match At A Nairobi Stadium

Football made in Kenya is a sight to behold! You will be entertained both by the players and their enthusiastic fans, many of whom paint themselves with the colours of the team they are supporting. Tip: Visit the Kenya Premier League website (kpl.co.ke) to see when matches are being played in the Nairobi stadiums, mainly Nyayo Stadium in Langata, City Stadium or Kasarani Stadium.

40. Shop At The Junction

The Junction is located along Ngong Road and has numerous shops from which you can shop, including a shop by Kitengela Glass where you can buy beautiful glass items. You can buy pizza or any other kind of fast food from the food court and go shopping at the Nakumatt supermarket. You can watch a movie at the state of the art movie theatre.

41. Go Boat Riding At Uhuru Park

Uhuru Park is a well tended area with trees and expansive lawns that add a green and relaxing touch to the hustle and bustle aura of Nairobi. You can go boat riding on Uhuru Park's artificial lake as you go by the foot bridges that adorn the park. Afterwards, you can picnic by one of the monuments dotting the park then immortalize your visit by having your photo taken by one of the many photographers in the park.

42. See Where Fierce Mau Mau Fighters Hid

Along the Oloolua forest nature trail that meanders through forest vines and indigenous bushes and trees, close to the Mbagathi river, you will see a 33 metre long cave. Inside this subterranean world are many underground caverns which are said to have been home to the Mau Mau freedom fighters during the colonial era. Tip: Carry a flashlight because it's dark in there!

43. See City Park's 900 Species Of Fauna And Flora

At Nairobi City Park, you can explore over 900 species of plants and animals, including many trees that are unique to Kenya. You can also visit a public cemetery where Pio Gama Pinto, an assassinated journalist and politician who fought for Kenya's independence, is buried. Adjacent to the cemetery is Murumbi Peace Memorial Park where Kenya's second vice president and his wife are buried.

44. Go Camping At Rowallan Camp

Rowallan Camp is adjacent to Ngong Road and offers a peaceful and relaxing setting for nature lovers. Water, hot showers, firewood for a campfire, nature trails, a swimming pool and for those who want to skip cooking, a cafeteria, are all provided. You can also hike to some caves which are in the Ngong Road Forest Reserve, where you will have to crawl on your stomach to enter since the entrance to the caves is quite small!

Mildred Achoch

Jogoo la shamba haliwiki mjinia

(The village cock does not crow in the city)

– Swahili Proverb

Mildred Achoch

45. See Parts of Nairobi While Running

Kenya is home to world-renowned athletics champions and you can sample a little bit of this Kenyan spirit during the monthly Parklands Sports Club run, which takes place on the first Sunday of every months from 7.30am. It is a fast-paced 15 kilometre road race through the Parklands, Westlands and Kilimani areas of Nairobi. Refreshments will be provided to everyone after the race and the winners receive prizes from the sponsors of the event.

46. Get Classy At The Concours D'elegance

The Concours d'Elegance is organized by the Alfa Romeo Owners Club and during this highly attended event, classic and vintage cars plus motorcycles will be judged under the regulations approved by Kenya Motor Sports Federation. There is also live band music, fly pasts and a grand parade of all the vintage and classy cars and motorcycles. Tip: Women enjoy dressing up for the event so come dressed in your best finery!

47. Take Part In The Stanchart Nairobi Marathon

If you will be in Nairobi towards the end of October, then you should take part in the Standard Chartered Bank of Kenya Nairobi Marathon. You have the choice of taking part in the 42 kilometre full marathon, the 21 kilometre half marathon or the 10 kilometre road race. In the 42 kilometre full marathon, you will run through various streets in the Central Business District then go up Museum Hill and through parts of Parklands then go back to Uhuru Highway and Mombasa road.

48. Watch Scrap Metal Artisans At Kamukunji

The jua kali (hot sun) artisans are a sight to behold as they bang scrap metal into shape, in concert, under the hot sun. Watch as they make items such as jikos (stoves), metal boxes, blacksmith tools, washing basins, pans, ladles, sufurias (cooking pots), gutters and other small items. Tip: Ask a local to accompany you so that you do not get lost.

49. Take A Break At The Jeevanjee Gardens

The Jeevanjee Gardens were founded by an Asian-born business man known as Alibhai Mulla Jeevanjee. It was donated to the people of Nairobi and is now a popular resting place. If you want to see the diversity of Nairobi, then Jeevanjee is the place to be because this is where Nairobians from all walks of life gather to rest, talk, play, preach and pray.

50. View Nairobi From The KICC

Nairobi has many vantage points where one can look at this green city's skyline but none of them compares to the rooftop of Nairobi's most recognizable landmark, the KICC – Kenyatta International Conference Centre. KICC is a 30 storey building that was built from the late 60s to the early 70s and its rooftop also doubles as the helipad. On weekdays, you can access the rooftop from 9am to 8pm and on weekends you can access it from 9am to 6pm.

Mildred Achoch

Top Reasons to Book This Trip

- Affordable: All the prizes are pocket friendly.
- Convenience: All the locations are relatively near to each other.
- Diverse Cultures: African, European, Indian and Arabic culture all converge in Nairobi.

Mildred Achoch

> TOURIST

GREATER THAN A TOURIST

Visit GreaterThanATourist.com
http://GreaterThanATourist.com

Sign up for the Greater Than a Tourist
Newsletter
http://eepurl.com/cxspyf

Follow us on Facebook:
https://www.facebook.com/GreaterThanATouri
st

Follow us on Pinterest:
http://pinterest.com/GreaterThanATourist

Follow us on Instagram:
http://Instagram.com/GreaterThanATourist

Mildred Achoch

> TOURIST

GREATER THAN A TOURIST

Please leave your honest review of this book on Amazon and Goodreads. Thank you.

We appreciate your positive and negative feedback as we try to provide tourist guidance in their next trip from a local.

> TOURIST

GREATER THAN A TOURIST

You can find Greater Than a Tourist books on Amazon.

Mildred Achoch

> TOURIST

GREATER THAN A TOURIST

WHERE WILL YOU TRAVEL TO NEXT?

Mildred Achoch

> TOURIST

GREATER THAN A TOURIST

Our Story

Traveling is a passion of this series creator. She studied abroad in college, and for their honeymoon Lisa and her husband toured Europe. During her travels to Malta, an older man tried to give her some advice based on his own experience living on the island since he was a young boy. She thought he was just trying to sell her something. When traveling to some places she was wary to talk to locals because she was afraid that they weren't being genuine. She created this book series to give you as a tourist an inside view on the place you are exploring and the ability to learn what locals would like to tell tourist. A topic that they are very passionate about.

Mildred Achoch

> TOURIST

GREATER THAN A TOURIST

Notes

Printed in Great Britain
by Amazon

17845989R00058